BRI REECE

Angry World

Understanding the Root Causes of Anger

This book is for anyone who has ever lost their temper and felt ashamed afterward. I have been there. I know what it feels like to react and then regret it. Be gentle with yourself. Anger does not make you broken. It means something inside you needs healing. You can always learn a better way to respond, to communicate, and to choose peace.
-Bri Reece

Contents

Introduction

Anger Is Human

Before we try to silence anger, suppress it, fix it, or condemn it, we have to be honest about what it actually is. Anger is a natural human emotion. Each one of us is capable of getting angry. It is not rare, and it is certainly not proof that you are broken or beyond repair. It is an emotion, just like joy, grief, fear, or love, and like every emotion it carries information about what is happening beneath the surface. The real issue has never been the existence of anger itself. The real issue is that most of us were never taught how to understand it, process it, or channel it in a healthy way. I do not remember anyone ever sitting me down and explaining how to manage anger. No one modeled what it looked like to feel it without being controlled by it. So like many people, I learned by reacting instead of reflecting.

In my early twenties and thirties, I would not have described myself as an angry person. I did not think of myself as someone with a problem. From my perspective, I simply had a short fuse. I believed certain people knew how to push my buttons, and I felt completely justified when I reacted. Disrespect, in my mind, required a response, and I was more than willing to deliver one. Crossing a line meant I had the right to explode, and at the time that explosion felt powerful. It felt necessary and made me feel strong. What I did not understand back then was that my reactions were not just about the moment in front of me. They were layered with older pain, unresolved disappointments, and experiences I had never slowed down long enough to examine. Anger was not starting in the present; it was being fueled by the past.

Looking around now, it is clear that this struggle is not personal just to me. We live in a culture that feels perpetually on edge. Scroll through social media for five minutes and you will see grown adults fighting in public spaces, screaming at customer service workers, or raging over minor inconveniences. Viral videos capture people losing control in grocery stores, airports, parking lots, and school events. It is easy to watch those clips and shake your head, wondering what is wrong with people. It is much harder to pause and ask what is driving that level of reactivity. Beneath most visible anger is something more vulnerable. There is often hurt, humiliation, fear, exhaustion, or a deep sense of powerlessness hiding under the surface. When we begin to ask what is underneath instead of simply condemning what we see, the conversation around anger shifts from judgment to understanding.

Anger does not usually begin where it finally explodes. It root source happens much earlier in life. It begins in childhood experiences that were never processed. It begins in moments of humiliation that were never addressed. It begins in abandon- ment, betrayal, fear, neglect, abuse, or feeling powerless. Over time, those experiences create a reservoir of emotion. When something in the present moment touches that old wound, the reaction can be explosive. The person reacting may not even realize they are responding to years of accumulated hurt rather than just the situation in front of them.

For a long time, I continued to refer to myself as an angry person. I wore it like a personality trait. That label became convenient because it excused my behavior. If I lost my temper, I could shrug and say, that is just how I am. The truth is, that identity was limiting me. The more I claimed anger as part of who I was, the more I gave it permission to lead my life I had indeed been through a lot at a young age, having a drug addict mother and a alcoholic father but I did not know that had anything to due with my anger.

This book is not here to shame you if anger has been part of your story. It is not here to pretend that people do not provoke, disrespect, betray, manipulate, or mistreat others. Some anger makes complete sense. There are situations in life that are genuinely unjust. There are wounds that cut deeply. There are moments when something inside you rises up because a boundary was crossed or a truth was violated. Anger often grows out of very real trauma, very real disappointment, and very real pain. Acknowledging that does not make you weak; it makes you honest.

What this book will challenge, gently but firmly, is the quiet belief that being justified in your anger gives you unlimited permission in how you express that anger. Feeling anger and acting on it destructively are two very different things. You may not always control the initial wave that rises in your chest. You may not be able to stop your heart from racing or your thoughts from flooding in when something unfair happens. What you absolutely can control is what happens next. That space between feeling and action is where growth lives. That space is where character is formed.

Life will continue to present situations that have the potential to make you explode with anger. People will misunderstand you, and some will intentionally try to hurt you. Others will disappoint you without even realizing they have done so. None of that is optional because we can not control other people. What is optional is whether you allow those moments to drag you into reactions that damage your peace, your relationships, or your future. Being responsible for your response does not mean you excuse harmful behavior. It means you refuse to let someone else's dysfunction determine your conduct.

There is a powerful shift that happens when you stop asking, "How dare they?" and start asking, "Who do I want to be in this moment?" That shift does not minimize your feelings. It honors them while also elevating you above them. You can acknowledge that something hurt you without turning that hurt into a weapon. You can also recognize injustice without becoming destructive. Responsibility for your reaction is not a burden placed on you; it is a form of freedom. It means your character is not at the mercy of circumstance.

Anger will visit every human being at some point. The lesson is not to deny its presence but to learn from it. Every triggering situation becomes an opportunity to practice self-mastery. Every moment of provocation becomes a chance to pause and decide whether you will escalate or evolve. No matter what has happened to you, no matter how justified you feel, you are still accountable for what you choose to do with that fire once it is lit. That is where the real transformation begins.

There was a moment in my life when I realized how dangerous unchecked anger can be. I owned a hair salon for thirty years. It was something I built from the ground up with folding tables and borrowed chairs. I had an employee who constantly showed up late and treated clients with a level of disrespect that embarrassed me. I addressed it calmly many times to her. I gave her many warnings. I tried to be patient with her and other that had similar personalities. One day during a staff meeting, her tone crossed the line of respect. She spoke to me in a way that felt deliberately disrespectful in front of the entire team.

In that moment, I felt something shift inside of me. I attempted to grab a decorative statue and lung toward her. I can still see it clearly. I can still feel the heat that rushed through my body. It literally looked like her face was illuminated in a red aura. By thank God, I stopped before I did something that would have destroyed everything I had worked for. Had I hit her, I could have lost my business, my reputation, and possibly my freedom. That moment forced me to confront something I had been avoiding for years. My anger was not under control. It was controlling me.

The next day, I called around the city looking for an anger management class. Most of the programs were designed for people who had been court mandated. I was not required by law to attend. I chose to go because I knew I was standing at a crossroads. Even though I was still quite young I knew that explosive behavior was not a good things. I found a class with a man named Dr. Young for sixty dollars an hour, I began learning tools that should have been taught much earlier in life. I began to understand that anger is often a secondary emotion. Beneath it there is usually fear, hurt, embarrassment, insecurity, or grief.

Another painful but important lesson came through my relationship with my daughter when she was seventeen. She had a sharp tongue. I was raised in a very old school environment where disrespect from a child was not tolerated. Our arguments became unhealthy. There were moments I am not proud of. I had to learn that even when I believed I was justified in my anger, I was still responsible for how i reacted to her. She was a child who was learning and growing. I was the adult who was responsible to teach her how to maintain control. That realization humbled me in a way nothing else could.

There are people sitting in prison today because of a single moment of uncontrolled anger. There are families fractured because someone reacted instead of pausing. There are careers ended because of one outburst. When we say we live in an angry world, we are not exaggerating. The stakes are real. The consequences are permanent.

At the same time, there is hope. Anger is not a life sentence. It is not a permanent identity. You are not required to carry rage for the rest of your life because of what happened to you in your past. There are root causes. There are tools. There are daily practices that can calm your nervous system and help you respond instead of react. There is help available if you are willing to seek it.

This book will guide you through understanding where anger comes from, how trauma shapes emotional responses, and how to take responsibility for your behavior without drowning in shame. We will talk about the difference between feeling anger and being ruled by it. We will explore practical techniques to interrupt destructive reactions. Most importantly, we will uncover the root so you can heal it instead of just trimming the surface.

If everyone in this world took the time to examine the source of their anger, to process the pain that fuels it, and to learn how to respond with clarity instead of impulse, our communities would look very different. Fewer fights. Fewer broken relationships. Fewer ruined lives. Collective healing begins with individual responsibility.

You do not have to identify as an angry person anymore. You

can choose who you are becoming each day, and that choice begins with understanding, not judgment.

Welcome to Angry World.

1

The Anger I Did Not Understand

For a long time, I believed I was simply wired differently. I told myself I had a strong personality, that I was passionate, that I did not tolerate disrespect. What I did not say out loud was that I was angry almost all the time. I was raised to be polite by my grandmother Ella Mae, so I was not rude but anger sat just beneath the surface, ready to rise at the smallest provocation. I reacted quickly and I spoke sharply to those that offended me. I defended myself before anyone's attack had even fully landed. At the time, I thought that tough behavior made me strong. Looking back, I see that I was carrying something much deeper than strength. I was carrying unresolved pain that I had never examined.

When people describe anger, they often talk about temper or attitude. They rarely talk about grief. They rarely talk about abandonment which made you feel unloved. They rarely talk about trauma that was never processed because the person experiencing it was too young to even understand what was happening. Anger became my armor long before I understood what I was protecting.

My biological mother was a drug addict. When I was three months old, during one of her drug binges, she placed me inside a suitcase and closed it. She said I cried too much as a baby. She attempted to take my life by putting that suitcase into the ocean. I survived thank God and my beloved grandmother who took me home and raised me as her own. She was my fathers mother from Dallas Texas. She took me and my older sister home and raised us with all the love she had in her. For most of my childhood and early adulthood, I did not walk around consciously thinking about that story. I buried it in the back of my mind. It existed in the background like a distant memory. I told it as a shocking fact sometimes after I became a motivational speaker, but I did not sit with what it meant.

What does it mean for a child to grow up knowing that the person who gave birth to them did not want them? What does it do to the nervous system of a human being to know that their life was almost ended before it even began? Those questions did not cross my mind in my twenties. I simply moved through life reacting. I did not connect the abandonment to the anger until much later in my life. Nor did I connect the early trauma to the sharpness in my voice. I definitely never connect the constant readiness to fight to the fear of being hurt again.

My grandmother became my world in every way a child needs someone to be. She was the one who wanted me, who chose me, who made sure my sister and I felt loved and safe. She took us to church and filled our lives with her old-school morals and values. She believed in structure, in discipline, in doing what was right even when it was hard. She raised me with consistency and care. She corrected me when I was wrong and comforted me when I was hurting. In every way that truly mattered, she was my parent. She was "Mama," the steady presence in a life that had already known too much instability.

When I was seventeen years old, that stability was ripped away in the most violent way imaginable. In May of 1987, I stood there and watched my grandfather, her husband of thirty-two years, shoot her in the head. The woman who had saved me, who had given me structure and protection, was taken from me in an instant in a horrible tragic way. There are moments in life that divide everything into before and after, and that was mine. That was the day my entire life changed. Something inside of me broke that day in a way I did not have the language to describe. My sense of safety collapsed. I lost all hope in God and humanity. My trust in people cracked wide open.

Life did not slow down to give me time to process what had happened. Thirty days later at seventeen years old, I put on a cap and gown and graduated from Centennial High School in Compton, California. I walked across that stage carrying shock and devastation beneath a composed exterior. No one teaches you how to metabolize that kind of trauma and pain. No one tells you how to hold grief that violent and still function as if everything is normal. I was expected to keep going, so I did.

My father had already died when I was ten, and my mother was still struggling with drug addiction. The safety net was now gone. In many ways, I began adulthood long before I was prepared for it. At nineteen, I got married without the life skills or emotional tools I truly needed. I was now a wife and I did not understand partnership or healthy communication yet. I was stepping into a role that required stability while carrying a heart filled with unprocessed trauma and what I now recognize as PTSD. At the time, I did not call it that. I did not say I was grieving or traumatized or afraid. Therapy was not something anyone suggested. Survival was the only goal, and survive is what I did.

Instead of acknowledging the depth of my pain, I labeled myself as someone with a very broken and had a bad temper. I told myself that I simply refused to be disrespected. I convinced myself that my sharp edges were part of my personality. Anger felt strong and safe, and strength felt necessary. Sadness felt dangerous because it required vulnerability, and vulnerability felt like exposure. Somewhere deep inside, my nervous system had learned that if I did not defend myself quickly and forcefully, I could be blindsided again. I could lose everything again. I could be left alone again.

What I did not understand then is that anger is often a secondary emotion. It rises to the surface because it feels more powerful than what lies beneath it. Under my anger lived severe grief that had never been expressed, fear that had never been soothed, and abandonment that had never been healed. The anger served as armor for me. It kept people at a distance and created the illusion of control. But armor is heavy, it weighs you down. Living in a constant state of defense exhausts the body and hardens the heart. I was not an angry person at my core; I was a wounded one. Until I was willing to look beneath the surface, that wound continued to shape how I moved through the world.

In my early twenties and thirties, I did not see the connection between my past and my present behavior. I built businesses. I worked hard. I was ambitious. On the outside, I looked productive. On the inside, I was constantly bracing for something to go wrong. When employees disappointed me, when relationships felt unstable, when someone's tone felt disrespectful, my reactions were amplified by years of stored emotion.

I did not wake up one morning and decide to be an angry person. I became one gradually, through unprocessed experiences and repeated defensive reactions. Each outburst reinforced the identity. Each justification strengthened the story that my anger was necessary.

It took a breaking point for me to pause and look deeper. It took a moment where my reaction almost cost me everything for me to ask myself an honest question. Why am I this angry? That question did not lead to immediate clarity. It led to discomfort. It led to revisiting memories I had tucked away. It led to acknowledging that my anger was not random. It had roots.

If you are reading this and you recognize yourself in any of it, I want you to hear something clearly. You are not crazy or defective in any way. You are not doomed to be angry forever. There is usually a story behind the rage. There is usually a wound behind the explosion. Understanding that does not excuse harmful behavior, but it does create a path toward healing.

Anger is not always about what is happening in front of you. Sometimes it is about what happened years ago and was never given space to be processed. Sometimes it is about feeling unwanted, unsafe, or unseen. Sometimes it is about survival instincts that never learned how to power down.

The moment I began connecting my abandonment and my trauma to my emotional responses, everything started to shift. Not overnight. Not perfectly. Slowly and deliberately. Awareness was the first step. Without awareness, anger feels like your personality. With awareness, it becomes something you can examine, understand, and eventually manage.

This chapter is not here to shock you with my story. It is here to show you that anger often makes sense once you trace the root of it back far enough. You may not have been placed in a suitcase like me. You may not have witnessed violence. Your story may look completely different from mine. The details change but the pattern remains the same. Unresolved pain has a way of resurfacing throughout your life.

You cannot heal what you refuse to name. You cannot regulate what you do not understand. The world may be angry, but you do not have to carry that anger as your identity for the rest of your life.

The roots matter, and we are going to dig them up together.

2

When Anger Becomes an Identity

There is a dangerous shift that happens when anger moves from being something you feel to something you believe you are. The emotion slowly turns into an identity. Instead of saying, I was angry in that moment, you begin saying, I am an angry person. That subtle difference shapes everything. Once anger becomes part of how you define yourself, it starts influencing your expectations, your reactions, and even the way other people treat you.

For years, I referred to myself that way. I would laugh about it sometimes. I would warn people. I would say, "You know I have a temper, plus I'm a Leo" That label felt honest at the time. It felt like I was owning who I was. In reality, I was reinforcing a pattern. Each time I repeated that statement, I gave anger permission to stay. I excused my sharp responses because I had already decided that was just my personality.

The truth is, identity is powerful. What you repeatedly call yourself becomes familiar. What becomes familiar becomes comfortable. Even when it is destructive, it can still feel normal. I had grown so accustomed to reacting quickly and forcefully that calm felt unnatural. Pausing felt weak. Letting something roll off my shoulders felt foreign. Anger was predictable. It was a reaction I knew how to execute.

What I did not realize was how exhausting it is to live in a constant state of readiness. When anger becomes part of your identity, your body never fully relaxes. Your nervous system stays alert. You interpret neutral situations as threats. A tone of voice feels like disrespect. A simple mistake feels intentional. You become hyper aware of anything that resembles the pain you have experienced before.

Looking back, I can see how abandonment shaped that identity. Somewhere deep inside, I believed I had to protect myself at all costs. I believed I could not afford to appear vulnerable. Anger became the shield. It told the world that I was not to be messed with. It created distance so that no one could get close enough to hurt me the way I had been hurt before.

The problem with building your identity around anger is that it begins to leak into every relationship. It shows up at work. It shows up at home. It shows up in friendships. It shows up in parenting. You may believe you are simply being strong or assertive, but the people around you often experience something very different. They feel tension. They feel unpredictability. They feel like they are walking on eggshells.

I had to face that reality in my own life. My employees did not just see me as a hardworking business owner. Some of them saw a boss whose mood could shift quickly. My daughter did not just see a mother who loved her deeply. She experienced someone who could react sharply when challenged. Even when I believed my frustration was justified, I had to admit that my responses were shaping the emotional climate around me.

There is a difference between having standards and having a short fuse. There is a difference between setting boundaries and exploding. I confused those things for a long time. I told myself I was simply not tolerating nonsense. In truth, I was allowing old wounds to dictate present reactions.

Once anger becomes your identity, you stop questioning it. You stop investigating it. You stop asking where it came from. Instead, you defend it. You explain it. You justify it. That defense mechanism keeps you stuck because you cannot change what you insist on protecting.

I remember the first time I seriously considered that I might not actually be an angry person at my core. That idea felt almost disorienting. If I was not naturally short tempered, then what was happening? If anger was not simply who I was, then it must have been something I learned or developed. That realization was uncomfortable because it meant I was responsible for unlearning it.

Responsibility can feel heavy, but it is also freeing. If anger is your personality, then you are trapped. If anger is a learned response to unresolved pain, then there is hope. Learned responses can be reworked. Habits can be interrupted. Patterns can be changed.

You are not born labeling yourself as angry. You become that version of yourself through repeated reactions. Each time you respond with aggression instead of reflection, you strengthen that neural pathway. Each time you pause and choose a calmer response, you begin carving a new one. The brain is adaptable. The nervous system can be retrained. Identity is not fixed.

When I began examining my own story honestly, I saw how

much unprocessed grief I had buried. I saw how much fear of abandonment I still carried. I saw how much anger was actually sadness wearing armor. That understanding did not excuse my past behavior, but it explained it. And explanation creates room for change.

You do not have to keep introducing yourself to the world through your anger. You do not have to preface your personality with warnings. You can decide that anger is something you feel occasionally rather than something you are permanently.

Letting go of that identity does not mean suppressing emotion. It means separating who you are from what you feel. You are not your anger. You are a human being who has experienced pain. That distinction matters because it gives you space to grow.

There is a quiet strength in saying, I used to react that way, but I am learning something different now. Growth rarely happens loudly. It happens in moments where you catch yourself before you explode. It happens when you recognize the heat rising in your body and choose to breathe instead of lash out. It happens when you refuse to let your past dictate your present.

If you have carried the identity of being "an angry person" for years, I want you to pause before you accept that as permanent truth. Labels have a way of sinking into our bones, shaping how we see ourselves and how we move through the world. After a while, you stop questioning them. You stop asking where they came from. You begin to believe that anger is simply who you are instead of something you learned to use. This is your moment to gently challenge that belief.

No child enters the world enraged at life. Babies cry because they need something. Toddlers scream because they lack language. Somewhere along the way, repeated hurt, disappointment, fear, neglect, betrayal, or instability teaches a person that intensity is safer than vulnerability. Anger becomes armor. It becomes a shield that feels stronger than sadness. It feels more powerful than fear. It disguises grief and makes you feel in control when everything else once felt chaotic.

Instead of condemning yourself for your reactions, begin by getting curious about them. Think back to when you first remember feeling that sharp edge inside you. Was it during childhood? Adolescence? After a particular relationship ended? After a loss you never properly processed? Trace it back, not to blame anyone, but to understand yourself. Growth does not start with shame. It starts with honest reflection.

Offer yourself compassion as you ask these questions. There is a reason you responded the way you did. There is a story behind every outburst, every slammed door, every cutting remark. Anger often develops as a survival strategy. It protects a younger version of you who did not feel safe, heard, or valued. That part of you may still be operating even though the original threat is long gone.

Consider what you might have been protecting all those years. Were you guarding against feeling abandoned again? Were you shielding yourself from rejection? Were you trying to avoid the humiliation of not being chosen or prioritized? When you look beneath the surface, anger frequently covers fear of being insignificant or invisible. Once you identify that underlying emotion, the intensity begins to make sense.

I want you to imagine sitting across from your younger self. Picture the age when you first remember feeling misunderstood or wounded. Instead of judging that version of you, speak to them gently. Ask what they needed at that time. Ask what they were afraid of. Most likely, you will discover that they were trying to survive circumstances that felt overwhelming. The adult you have become can now offer the reassurance they never received.

Understanding this does not excuse harmful behavior, but it reframes it. There is a difference between accountability and self-condemnation. Taking responsibility for your reactions is necessary, yet beating yourself up for having them keeps you stuck. Real transformation happens when you acknowledge both the pain that shaped you and the power you now have to respond differently.

It is important to recognize that anger can feel energizing. It can provide a false sense of strength. When you have felt powerless in the past, anger creates the illusion of control. Letting go of that familiar intensity may feel uncomfortable at first because it means allowing yourself to feel softer emotions you once avoided. Sadness, disappointment, loneliness, and grief may surface. That does not mean you are regressing. It means you are healing.

Take time to reflect on patterns in your life. Notice if certain comments or behaviors consistently ignite you. Ask yourself what those triggers have in common. Do they touch on themes of disrespect, abandonment, criticism, or comparison? Identifying patterns reveals that your reactions are not random. They are connected to unresolved experiences that still carry emotional weight.

Another powerful question to ask is this: Who taught me that anger was the appropriate response? Perhaps you grew up in a household where yelling was normal. Maybe you watched adults use intimidation to get their way. When that environment becomes your blueprint, you unconsciously repeat it. Awareness gives you the opportunity to break that cycle.

Offer yourself patience during this process. Years of conditioning will not unravel overnight. The goal is not to become someone who never feels anger. The goal is to understand it well enough that it no longer controls you. Healthy anger can signal that a boundary has been crossed. Destructive anger erupts without reflection and damages relationships. Learning the difference requires ongoing self-examination.

You deserve the same empathy you would extend to a friend. If someone you loved confided in you about their trauma and explosive reactions, you would not tell them they are hopeless. You would encourage them to look at what happened and to seek healing. Extend that same grace inward. Compassion does not make you weak. It creates the safe internal space needed for growth.

Reflect on how your life might change if you stopped introducing yourself to yourself as an angry person. Imagine seeing yourself instead as someone who experienced deep pain and is actively working to transform it. That subtle shift alters your identity. You move from resignation to possibility. You begin to believe that change is attainable.

There may be grief involved in this realization. You might feel sadness for the years spent reacting instead of responding. You might regret relationships strained by unmanaged emotion. Allow yourself to feel that grief without dwelling in it. Regret can either paralyze you or motivate you. Choose to let it fuel your commitment to doing better moving forward.

Anger often masks unmet needs. Spend time identifying what those needs were and whether they are still relevant. Did you crave affirmation, stability, affection, or safety? As an adult, you now have tools and resources that were unavailable to you as a child. Meeting those needs in healthy ways diminishes the urgency that once drove your reactions.

Remember that transformation begins with awareness but is sustained through practice. Each time you pause before reacting, you reinforce a new pattern. Each time you choose calm over chaos, you weaken the old identity you once accepted. Change is built moment by moment through conscious decisions.

There is tremendous strength in acknowledging your past without allowing it to dictate your future. Understanding what happened to you does not trap you there. It frees you from unconscious repetition. When you look at your anger with curiosity instead of condemnation, you remove its mystery and reduce its power.

You are not defined by your worst reaction. You are defined by your willingness to evolve. The person who once relied on anger to feel safe can learn healthier ways to navigate discomfort. That evolution begins with a simple but profound shift: replacing harsh self-judgment with compassionate inquiry.

As you move forward, continue asking yourself gentle, honest questions. What am I feeling beneath this anger? What old wound is being touched? What would a calmer version of me choose right now? Those questions build self-awareness and self-control simultaneously.

An angry world needs individuals who are brave enough to heal their own stories. When you understand the origin of your reactions, you reduce the amount of unprocessed pain you project onto others. That ripple effect matters more than you realize.

You were not born angry. You were shaped by experiences that left marks. Those marks can be addressed. They can be softened. They can even become sources of wisdom. Begin by extending compassion to yourself and asking what truly happened. That is where the healing starts.

Anger may have served a purpose at one point. It may have helped you survive. It may have kept you guarded when you needed protection. Survival strategies are not meant to become permanent personalities. Once you are safe enough to reflect, you have the opportunity to choose differently.

You are not locked into who you were at your lowest moments. You are allowed to evolve. You are allowed to heal. You are allowed to separate your identity from your reactions.

Anger is an emotion. It is not your name.

3

Triggers, Trauma, and the Moment You See Red

There was a time in my life when I truly believed my temper was part of my personality. I did not hide it. I actually bragged about it. Overreacting to situations, ranting to make my point, raising my voice so everyone understood I was serious, those behaviors felt normal to me. I convinced myself that intensity meant strength and that my anger made people respect me. Looking back, I can see that what I was really doing was masking something much deeper.

Running a business only amplified the issue. As a salon owner, I believed that in order to keep my staff in line I had to be strict, dominant, and occasionally explosive. If someone broke one of my very detailed rules, I felt justified in reacting strongly. I even joked that it was because I am a Leo, as if astrology explained away my inability to regulate my emotions. It became easy to laugh it off instead of examining it.

Over time, something began to shift my mindset. I started noticing a difference between employees who followed the rules because they respected me and those who followed them because they were afraid of me. Fear produces compliance, but it does not produce loyalty or love. Respect grows from consistency, fairness, and calm leadership. I had convinced myself that dictatorship was effective, but in truth it was isolating. My outbursts were not strengthening my authority. They were weakening my influence. I truly am a great loving person at heart but my unhealed trauma kept me misguided and afraid to get close to people.

The breaking point came during a staff meeting that I have already mentioned briefly in the introduction. I had nine employees at the time, and I was overwhelmed. Running a business where your name is on the building means that every mistake becomes your responsibility. If someone showed up late, I had to apologize to clients. If someone delivered poor service, I had to offer discounts. The pressure was constant, and my patience was getting thin. Especially since I had detail, mapped out rules for them to follow. I trained them how to speak pleasantly to clients and how to resolve conflict in the salon.

During that staff meeting, I was addressing general concerns about tardiness, hygiene, and professionalism. I was trying to avoid singling anyone out. One particular employee kept interrupting me, asking repeatedly if I was talking about her. Her tone was sharp, rude and defensive. The more she pushed, the more my body reacted. It was as if something ancient and unhealed was being poked. At that time I had just begun the mental and emotional transformations journey.

People often describe anger as "seeing red," and that description is accurate. My vision actually shifted. Everything blurred to a hazy red, except for her face. I attempted reached for a small statue on my desk and made a motion as if I was going to throw it at her. For a split second, I lost control. Then instantly something stopped me. I sat back down. I took a breath. I fired her on the spot but calmly instead.

In that moment, I understood how close I had come to destroying everything I had worked for. I owned a home. I ran the largest Braiding and Dreadlock Salon in the city. One impulsive act could have cost me my business, my reputation, and possibly my freedom. That realization shook me deeply. I could no longer pretend that my anger was harmless or justified. It had escalated to a point where it was dangerous.

What I did next truly changed the direction of my life. Instead of continuing to justify my reactions or blaming other people for "pushing my buttons," I made a decision that humbled me. I searched for an anger management coach and found Dr. Young, a man who primarily worked with court-mandated clients. Most of the people sitting in his office were there because a judge had ordered them to be. I walked in because I chose to. That distinction mattered to me. Paying sixty dollars an hour for six weeks of one-on-one sessions forced me to acknowledge that this was not just a personality quirk. It was something serious enough to invest time, money, and ego into confronting. Later, I enrolled in another anger management program at West Los Angeles College because I wanted reinforcement. For the first time in my life, I was not reacting blindly. I was learning about triggers, nervous system responses, and emotional regulation in a structured way.

Sitting across from Dr. Young was not glamorous. It was very uncomfortable. He asked questions that peeled back layers I had spent years protecting. He explained that anger itself is not the first emotion; it is usually the second. Beneath it often sits hurt, fear, humiliation, or a sense of powerlessness. Research in behavioral psychology supports that idea. Studies show that nearly 80 percent of people report experiencing intense anger at least once a week, yet many struggle to identify the underlying feeling driving it. According to the American Psychological Association, chronic unmanaged anger is linked to increased risk of heart disease, high blood pressure, and anxiety disorders. That alone was sobering. The consequences were not just relational; they were physical. Statistics from road rage studies indicate that aggressive driving contributes to thousands of injuries annually, and in surveys conducted by the AAA Foundation, nearly 80 percent of drivers admitted to expressing significant anger, aggression, or road rage in the past year. The line between irritation and danger is thinner than most people think.

Learning about triggers reshaped the way I viewed my reactions. A trigger is not simply the event that happens in front of you. It is the meaning your nervous system attaches to that event based on your history. For years, I believed my anger was about lateness, tone, or attitude. In reality, those were surface details. What truly set me off were feelings of disrespect, abandonment, and dismissal. When someone walked out of a room while I was speaking, it was not just about poor manners. It activated something old and unresolved. When my teenage daughter spoke sharply to me, the reaction that surged through my body was larger than the moment required. The intensity came from wounds that had nothing to do with her and everything to do with experiences I had never fully processed.

Writing down my triggers was both painful and enlightening. Situations that seemed small from the outside carried enormous emotional weight for me. Being interrupted, being ignored, being told I was "too much," or feeling excluded could ignite a reaction that surprised even me. As I traced those triggers back, I saw clear connections to abandonment issues and struggles with self-worth that had followed me quietly for years. The overreactions were rarely about the present moment alone. They were echoes. They were old pain demanding attention in new environments.

Experts often explain that the brain's amygdala, the part responsible for detecting threat, can react in milliseconds, long before the rational part of the brain has time to evaluate what is actually happening. That biological speed explains why anger feels so explosive. One moment you are calm, and the next your heart is racing and your voice is raised. Without awareness and training, that reaction can override logic completely. In fact, neuroscientists describe something called an "amygdala hijack," where emotional response temporarily takes control of behavior before conscious reasoning catches up. Understanding that helped me realize I was not evil or out of control by design. I was untrained. I had never learned how to slow that process down.

Working with Dr. Young and attending those classes gave me tools to pause. Breathing techniques. Cognitive reframing. Recognizing early physical cues like tightened shoulders or a rising voice. The more I practiced, the more space I created between feeling and action. That space became everything. It allowed me to ask myself what I was truly reacting to before I spoke. It allowed me to consider whether the person in front of me was actually attacking me or whether my past was simply being replayed.

Looking back, voluntarily walking into anger management

was one of the most empowering decisions I have ever made. It required humility to admit that I needed help. It required courage to confront parts of myself that were uncomfortable. What it gave me in return was clarity. Anger stopped feeling like an uncontrollable force and started feeling like a signal I could interpret. Once I understood the root, the reaction began to lose its intensity.

Many people wait until consequences force them to address their temper. Arrest records, broken relationships, lost jobs, and fractured families are often the wake-up call. I am grateful that I chose to step in before my life was rearranged by a single uncontrolled moment. It does not take long to lose your temper. Research shows that most anger escalations happen within seconds. It only takes one unfiltered outburst to damage trust that took years to build. Understanding that truth sobers you quickly.

Examining my triggers honestly did not make me weak. It made me responsible. It helped me see that my anger was not random. It was patterned. It was connected. Once I saw that clearly, change stopped feeling impossible. It became intentional.

Understanding this did not excuse my behavior, but it gave me clarity. There will always be people who provoke us. There will always be circumstances that have the potential to ignite frustration. The world will not suddenly become perfectly calm and respectful. The only variable we truly control is our response.

Anger is not your friend. It does not protect your relationships. It does not build long term success. It can damage your physical health as well. I suffered from migraines and severe stomach ulcers during the height of my anger. I treated the physical symptoms with medication, never realizing that the true issue was internal. The body absorbs what the mind refuses to process.

Learning to pause became one of the most powerful tools I ever developed. Even a single second of reflection can change the course of an outcome. Instead of reacting immediately, I began asking myself what I was truly feeling underneath the anger. Was it embarrassment? Fear? Disappointment? Identifying the root emotion softened the reaction.

My father's story also played a role in shaping my emotional world. He loved my sister and me deeply, yet his addiction to alcohol controlled his life. He would promise to take us to the park, and we would wait on the porch, only to watch him arrive too intoxicated to follow through. That pattern created a sense of instability and disappointment that I carried into adulthood. When someone failed to meet my expectations, it triggered that same old feeling of being let down.

Death, addiction, abandonment, and trauma leave imprints. Not every instance of anger is rooted in childhood pain, but many are. If we do not examine those roots, we risk projecting unresolved hurt onto the people in our present lives.

I eventually met with my mother as an adult, carrying years of expectation into that encounter. I had imagined how the conversation would go. I believed it would bring closure. When reality did not match the script in my head, I felt another wave of disappointment. Healing requires releasing expectations and approaching those conversations with openness rather than rehearsed outcomes.

For a long time, I called myself broken and angry. I wore that label as armor. It kept people at a distance and gave me a false sense of control. What I now understand is that anger is often a signal. It points toward something that needs attention. When you take the time to identify your triggers and trace them back to their source, you begin to reclaim your power.

Every situation can be handled from a place of peace if you are willing to do the internal work first. That does not mean you become passive or silent. It means your response becomes intentional instead of impulsive.

If there are people in your past who contributed to your pain and you have the opportunity to communicate with them safely, consider doing so. If direct contact is not wise or possible, write a letter expressing your feelings without expecting a specific reaction. The purpose is not to change them. The purpose is to free yourself.

We are not destined to remain the wounded versions of ourselves. We are capable of growth, insight, and transformation. I had lived long enough as an angry person. Once I connected my triggers to my past and accepted responsibility for my reactions, I began moving toward peace.

Anger may explain your past behavior, but it does not have to define your future.

4

The Cost of Carrying It

For a long time, I believed my anger was protecting me. It felt like armor. It felt like strength. It felt like a warning sign to the world that I was not the little girl who had been abandoned, not the teenager who had watched her grandmother die, not the child who had waited on a porch for a father who loved her but could not choose her over alcohol. Anger made me feel powerful when underneath I felt deeply hurt.

What I did not understand then was how expensive that armor really was. Every outburst cost me something. Sometimes it cost me peace. Sometimes it cost me connection. Sometimes it cost me my own health. Those migraines that would knock me flat were not random. The stomach ulcers that left me doubled over were not simply the result of stress. My body was reacting to years of unprocessed emotion that I kept forcing down until it erupted.

There is a physical toll to unresolved anger. The body was not designed to live in a constant state of fight or flight. When your nervous system is always braced for disrespect, abandonment, or betrayal, it never gets the chance to rest. That constant internal tension begins to show up in subtle ways at first. Sleepless nights. Tight shoulders. Clenched jaws. Eventually it can evolve into something much more serious.

Beyond the physical cost, there is a relational cost that many of us do not notice until it is too late. When people are afraid of your reactions, they begin to withdraw. They share less. They become guarded. The very thing you fear, being left out, being disrespected, being abandoned, becomes more likely because your anger pushes others away. I had to face the painful truth that some of the distance I felt in my relationships had been created by my own explosive behavior.

The situation with my seventeen-year-old daughter forced me to see this clearly. She had a sharp mouth at times, and I was raised in a generation where children did not speak to adults in certain ways. Every time she challenged me, something inside me flared up. I felt disrespected, invalidated, and triggered. From my perspective, I was justified. From a deeper perspective, I was reacting from old wounds that had nothing to do with her teenage emotions.

Parenting requires emotional maturity. Even when a child is wrong, the adult is still responsible for how the situation is handled. I had to learn that my reaction would either escalate the conflict or calm it. Raising my voice did not teach her respect. Modeling emotional control did. That lesson was humbling, and it required me to confront parts of myself I had ignored for years.

Anger often disguises itself as righteousness. We tell ourselves that we are simply standing up for what is right. There are certainly moments when anger signals injustice and calls us to action. However, many of our daily explosions are not about justice. They are about ego, hurt, and fear. Without awareness, it becomes easy to confuse the two.

I also had to acknowledge how anger distorted my self-perception. Calling myself an "angry person" became a self-fulfilling identity. When you label yourself that way, you unconsciously look for opportunities to confirm it. You expect to lose your temper. You almost prepare for it. Breaking that pattern required me to stop identifying with the behavior and start identifying with the person I wanted to become.

Letting go of anger does not mean pretending that trauma never happened. It does not mean excusing the people who hurt you. It means deciding that their actions will not continue to control your present reactions. There is a difference between remembering your past and living from it every single day.

Healing began when I allowed myself to grieve honestly. I grieved the mother I did not have. I grieved the father I wished had been stronger than his addiction. I grieved the grandmother who raised me and was taken from me violently. Those layers of grief had hardened into anger because grief felt too vulnerable. Once I permitted myself to feel the sadness, the anger slowly began to loosen its grip.

Compassion for myself became part of the process. Instead of shaming myself for my temper, I began asking what it was trying to protect. That question shifted everything. Beneath the yelling and the sharp words was a woman who was afraid of being hurt again. Recognizing that softened my heart toward myself and toward others.

The world we live in today feels tense. Social media amplifies outrage. Public spaces sometimes erupt into chaos over minor disagreements. It can seem as though anger is the new normal.

Participating in that culture only deepens the divide. Choosing a different way to respond becomes an act of quiet rebellion.

There are people sitting in jail right now because they reacted in a single heated moment without pausing. There are families fractured beyond repair because no one was willing to lower their voice and listen. One impulsive decision can alter the trajectory of a life. When you truly understand that, the importance of self-control becomes undeniable.

Peace is not passive. It requires strength and demands self-awareness. It calls you to slow down when everything inside you wants to lash out. Developing that discipline does not make you weak. It makes you powerful in a way that anger never could.

As I continued in therapy and anger management, I learned practical tools. Deep breathing before responding. Walking away temporarily instead of escalating. Identifying physical cues that signaled I was becoming triggered. Practicing calmer communication even when I did not feel calm. Over time, those tools rewired my reactions.

The transformation was not immediate. There were still moments when I slipped. Growth is rarely linear. What changed was my commitment. I no longer excused my outbursts. I took responsibility for them. Each time I chose a calmer response, I strengthened a new habit.

Looking back, I see that anger was never truly about the present moment. It was about pain that had never been given a voice. Once that pain was acknowledged and processed, the intensity diminished.

Carrying anger is heavy. It exhausts you. It isolates you. It quietly erodes your health and your relationships. Putting it down does not mean you forget your story. It means you decide your story will not dictate your future behavior.

The cost of carrying it was too high for me. Choosing peace did not erase my past, but it gave me a different future. If you are reading this and recognizing yourself in these words, know that change is possible. Anger may have shaped parts of your life, but it does not have to shape the rest of it.

5

Holes

When I finally reached a place where I could open my mouth and tell the truth about my life, something surprising happened. I discovered that my story was not as isolated as I once believed. There were abandoned children sitting in grown bodies. There were adults walking around with undiagnosed PTSD, with trauma responses they did not understand, reacting to present situations with emotions that belonged to the past. For years I thought my anger meant I was defective or dramatic or simply "crazy," as some people casually labeled me. Once I began sharing honestly, I realized I was neither alone nor insane. I was wounded.

There are so many people moving through this angry world carrying unresolved pain, trying to hold it together without ever seeking help, sometimes not even knowing help exists. They go to work. They raise families. They smile in public. Meanwhile, something inside them is leaking. That is why this chapter belongs in this book. If we are going to understand the root causes of anger, we have to talk about the holes.

I did not seriously begin confronting my issues until I was in my late thirties. That is a long time to live on autopilot, reacting from wounds you have never examined. My hope in sharing what I have learned is that someone else does not have to wait that long. Healing does not have to be delayed until you have already burned through relationships, opportunities, and your own peace.

Unfavorable life experiences create what I describe as holes. These are not physical holes that anyone can see. They are emotional and spiritual gaps formed by unresolved trauma, rejection, loss, and neglect. They are the places where something essential was torn away and never properly restored.

For years I walked around with enormous holes in my heart. I did not know that was what they were. I only knew that I felt intensely, reacted quickly, and often regretted the aftermath. As I grew older and more observant, I began to notice that many people were living with similar openings inside of them. Some carried wounds far deeper than mine. Some hid them better. Others wore them openly as anger, bitterness, sarcasm, or emotional distance.

If those holes are ignored, they do not stay small. Life keeps moving. Responsibilities pile up. New relationships begin. Children are born. Careers are built. On the surface everything appears normal, yet the untreated wounds quietly expand. They affect how we interpret innocent comments. They distort how we receive love. They interfere with how we give it. We were created to love naturally and without fear, but when love was denied early on, something fractures.

I have often felt as if tiny pieces of my soul slipped through those holes over the years. I did not consciously know I was trying to retrieve them, but that is exactly what I was doing every time I demanded reassurance, every time I overreacted to perceived rejection, every time I tried to control a situation so I would not feel abandoned again. During that process, I hurt people who had never intended to hurt me. At the time I could not see it. I only saw my own pain.

There were countless moments when I exploded and could not explain why the reaction felt so large compared to the situation. Friends and family were confused. They assumed I was simply hot-headed. What none of us understood was that they were not dealing with the present moment alone. They were encountering years of unresolved grief and abandonment erupting through a small trigger.

One afternoon at the mall, my ex-husband made a harmless comment about liking the way a pair of shoes looked on a woman who walked past us. His tone was casual. There was no flirtation, no insult, no disrespect intended. In a healthy emotional space, that remark would have floated by without consequence. Instead, the untreated holes in my heart translated his words into something completely different. I heard, "I wish you looked like her." I heard, "You are not enough." I heard confirmation of a fear that had lived inside me since childhood.

The reaction that followed was not about shoes. It was about insecurity rooted in abandonment. I went home, gathered every pair of shoes I owned, and threw them at him while screaming that if he liked her shoes so much he could have mine. Today we laugh about that scene because time and healing provide perspective. In that moment it was explosive and painful. I genuinely believed I was defending myself against rejection.

Growing up without a mother's love left a mark deeper than I realized. Even though I had people who loved me, I did not know how to receive that love fully because I had not learned to love myself. Until those holes were addressed, every relationship was at risk of being filtered through fear.

Another memory stands out clearly. I was eighteen years old, still grieving the murder of my grandmother who had raised me, trying to navigate life without the only stable parent I had ever known. My sister had gone off to college at UC San Diego. After our grandmother's funeral, I moved in with my Aunt SaBra, my father's sister. Our family felt small and fragile. We had already lost so much.

When my sister called to say she would not be coming home for Thanksgiving or Christmas, the news devastated me. Objectively, her decision made sense. She was adjusting to college life and working. It was a normal choice for a young adult. Emotionally, I interpreted it as another abandonment. I cried uncontrollably. I ranted. I accused her of leaving me behind. I felt as if the last person who understood my grief was disappearing too.

Looking back, I can see that her decision had nothing to do with rejecting me. She was grieving in her own way. She was building her life. My reaction came from the hole left by my mother's abandonment and deepened by my grandmother's death. Loss had become my expectation. Any sign of distance felt like confirmation that I was not worth staying for.

At the time, I could not articulate any of that. All I knew was that I felt alone and terrified of being left again. The erratic behavior that followed was rooted in fear, not in the present circumstance. It would take years before I connected those dots.

Once I began doing the internal work, I understood something life-changing. Because I had been abandoned, I did not feel valuable. That belief shaped my reactions more than I realized. Every perceived slight reinforced it. Every disagreement triggered it. Anger became my shield against feeling worthless.

Nothing shifts in our lives until we acknowledge our wounds. Physical injuries begin healing on their own with time. Emotional and psychological injuries require conscious attention. They do not close simply because years have passed. In fact, time can deepen them if they are repeatedly triggered.

If you are reading this and recognizing parts of yourself, I encourage you to identify your own holes. They may have been formed by abandonment, abuse, betrayal, neglect, addiction in the family, sudden loss, or chronic instability. The specifics differ, but the impact often looks similar: hypersensitivity, defensiveness, explosive reactions, or emotional withdrawal.

Finding a way to close those holes is not weakness. It is courage. For some people that means therapy. For others it means support groups, spiritual counseling, journaling, or difficult but necessary conversations. In certain cases, writing a letter to someone who hurt you can provide release even if you never send it. The goal is not confrontation for revenge. The goal is understanding and emotional closure.

When I chose to meet with my biological mother later in life, I made the mistake of entering that encounter with expectations about how she would respond. I hoped for remorse, clarity, perhaps an apology that would magically heal everything. That expectation set me up for disappointment. Healing cannot depend on someone else behaving the way we want them to. Closure is an internal decision.

Forgiveness became a turning point for me. Forgiving my mother did not mean excusing what happened. It meant releasing myself from the constant emotional grip of it. As I worked through that process, the massive hole I had grown accustomed to hiding began to shrink. I felt lighter. I reacted less explosively. My anger softened because its root was being addressed.

This chapter matters in a book called *Angry World* because much of the anger we see around us is not random. It is the visible symptom of invisible holes. People lash out because something inside them feels threatened, invalidated, or unseen. That does not excuse harmful behavior, but it does explain it.

When we understand that our anger may be leaking from old wounds, we gain power. Instead of asking only, "Why did they make me so mad?" we begin asking, "What inside of me was touched?" That question changes everything. It shifts us from blame to awareness.

Closing the holes does not happen overnight. It requires honesty, humility, and patience. The reward, however, is profound. As those openings seal, you regain pieces of yourself that felt lost. You stop bleeding onto people who never cut you. You respond from the present rather than from the past.

An angry world will not calm down until individuals begin healing their internal wounds. The work is personal. The responsibility is individual. The impact, however, is collective. When you close your holes, you reduce the anger you project into your family, your workplace, and your community.

The fire that once erupted from me did not disappear by accident. It softened because I was willing to look at the places where I had been broken. Understanding the root causes of my anger allowed me to respond differently. The same possibility exists for anyone willing to do the work.

6

Justified but Still Responsible

One of the hardest truths I had to accept on my journey was this: being justified in your anger does not give you permission to lose control. That realization humbled me deeply. For years, I believed that if someone disrespected me, lied to me, disappointed me, or crossed a clear boundary, my explosive reaction was understandable. In many cases, it was understandable. What I did not understand at the time was that understanding does not equal wisdom.

There is a difference between feeling anger and acting out of anger. The emotion itself is not the enemy. Anger is a signal. It alerts us that something feels wrong, unfair, or painful. The problem begins when we allow that signal to drive the car. When anger grabs the steering wheel, the outcome is rarely productive. It may feel powerful for a moment, but the aftermath usually leaves regret, damaged relationships, or consequences that cannot be undone.

Looking back at my younger years, I can see how often I reacted from a place of pain rather than clarity. When my employee spoke disrespectfully in that meeting, I was not just reacting to her tone. I was reacting to every time I had felt dismissed or invalidated in my life. When my daughter challenged me, I was not just correcting a teenager. I was responding to a deep fear of losing control or being disrespected again. The present moment was layered with unresolved history.

Understanding this does not excuse bad behavior from others. People will still be wrong sometimes. They will still lie. They will still disappoint you. They will still say things that sting. Recognizing the root of your anger is not about pretending that what happened was acceptable. It is about separating what happened from how you choose to respond to it.

Responsibility is the turning point. It is the moment you realize that although you did not choose your trauma, you are still accountable for your reactions. That truth can feel unfair at first. Why should you have to do the work when someone else caused the pain? The answer is simple, because your future depends on it. Holding on to uncontrolled anger only extends the damage long after the original event has passed.

There are people sitting behind prison walls today because they acted in a single heated moment without pausing. There are marriages that ended because neither person was willing to step back and lower their voice. There are children who grew up afraid in homes where adults could not regulate their tempers. One reaction can alter the trajectory of an entire life.

When I began to truly grasp this, I stopped seeing emotional control as optional. It became essential. I started asking myself a different question in heated moments. Instead of asking, "Am I right?" I began asking, "What will this reaction create?" That shift changed everything. Being right does not matter if the result is destruction.

Learning to pause does not mean suppressing your feelings. It means creating space between emotion and action. That space might be a deep breath. It might be stepping into another room. It might be deciding not to respond to a text message immediately. That small gap can be the difference between escalation and resolution.

There is also something powerful about acknowledging your anger without dramatizing it. Saying to yourself, "I am upset right now," is very different from shouting, "You always do this to me." The first statement centers you. The second one attacks and inflames the situation. Words matter. Tone matters. Timing matters.

I had to practice responding differently long before it felt natural. Calm leadership did not come easily to me in the beginning. It required intentional effort. During staff meetings, I began choosing a softer tone. I focused on clear communication instead of intimidation. Over time, I noticed something surprising. My employees responded better. They listened more carefully. They respected me not because they feared me, but because they felt valued.

The same shift occurred in my home. When I responded to my daughter with steadiness instead of heat, our conversations changed. She still made mistakes. She was still a teenager finding her voice. The difference was that I was no longer escalating the conflict. I was modeling the emotional maturity I wanted her to develop.

An angry world will not heal itself through louder voices and sharper words. It will heal through individuals who decide to regulate their emotions even when they feel provoked. That choice begins internally. It begins with understanding that your anger is information, not instruction.

There will always be triggers. There will always be days when your patience feels thin. The goal is not perfection. The goal is awareness and growth. Each time you choose a measured response instead of an explosive one, you strengthen a new pattern. That pattern eventually becomes your default.

If you have lived years identifying as an angry person, let me assure you that identity can change. I once believed my temper was simply who I was. Now I understand it was a response shaped by unresolved pain. Once the pain was addressed, the intensity softened.

You are allowed to feel what you feel. You are not required to let that feeling control your behavior. Taking responsibility for your reactions is not a burden. It is empowerment. It means you are no longer a slave to your triggers. It means you are capable of choosing the outcome you want instead of surrendering to impulse.

Justified anger can still destroy what you value most if left unchecked. Learning to respond consciously protects your relationships, your reputation, and your peace of mind. That lesson cost me years of turmoil before I embraced it. My hope is that you can learn it sooner and with less damage along the way.

7

The Anger Beneath the Anger

There is a layer of anger that most people see, and then there is the layer that lives underneath it. The top layer is loud. It raises its voice. It slams doors. It types angry comments online. It reacts quickly and often regrets just as quickly. Beneath that layer is something much quieter and much more vulnerable. Beneath that layer is hurt. Beneath that layer is fear. Beneath that layer is grief that was never fully processed.

For many years, I only knew the surface version of my anger. I knew how to defend myself. I knew how to speak sharply when I felt challenged. I knew how to make sure no one mistook my kindness for weakness. What I did not know was how deeply wounded I was. I did not realize that I had built my personality around protecting a little girl who once felt unwanted and unsafe.

When your biological mother tries to take your life at three months old because she says you cried too much, something is imprinted into your nervous system. Even if you do not consciously remember it, your body remembers. When that same child then grows up watching the woman who saved her, the grandmother who became her world, be murdered in front of her at seventeen years old, the psyche absorbs trauma that words cannot fully capture. For years, I carried that weight without fully understanding it.

I walked through my twenties and thirties reacting to life as if it were constantly threatening to take something from me. Any hint of disrespect felt like danger. Any sign of instability felt like the ground was about to fall away again. The anger I displayed was my attempt to regain control in a world that had once felt wildly uncontrollable.

What I know now is that unprocessed grief often disguises itself as rage. It is easier to be angry than it is to be brokenhearted. Anger feels powerful. Grief feels weak. Anger pushes people away before they can hurt you again. Grief requires you to admit that you were hurt and that it mattered deeply.

I had to sit with memories I had avoided for decades. I had to allow myself to feel the sadness of not having a mother who was healthy and present. I had to acknowledge the fear that came from watching violence steal the person who raised me. I had to admit that a part of me had been operating from survival mode ever since. That process was not comfortable. It was not quick. It was necessary.

When you begin to trace your anger back to its roots, you may discover that it is connected to moments that shaped your identity. Perhaps you were humiliated publicly as a child. Perhaps you grew up in a home where yelling was the only form of communication. Perhaps you learned early that vulnerability was punished. Those early experiences become templates. Without awareness, you replay them over and over in adulthood.

The world around us does not make this any easier. We are living in a time where outrage is rewarded. Social media platforms amplify conflict because conflict keeps people engaged. Fights break out at concerts and sporting events. Adults scream at each other over political differences. Road rage incidents escalate into violence. It can begin to feel normal, as if anger is simply the way things are now.

Normal does not mean healthy. Collective tension is often the result of millions of individuals who have not addressed their personal pain. If each person took the time to unpack their own wounds, the temperature of the world would drop significantly. That might sound idealistic, but I believe it with my whole heart.

The turning point in my own journey was recognizing that my anger was not protecting me anymore. It was isolating me. It was exhausting me. It was slowly eroding the peace I claimed I wanted. I had to make a decision about who I wanted to be. Did I want to continue identifying as an angry person, or did I want to become a healed one?

Healing does not erase the past. It does not rewrite what happened. It changes how you carry it. I began practicing daily reflection. I started noticing the physical cues that signaled I was being triggered. My chest would tighten. My jaw would clench. My thoughts would speed up. Instead of moving immediately into reaction, I began asking myself what was truly being activated.

Sometimes the answer surprised me. A simple disagreement would bring up a memory of feeling unheard as a child. A delayed response from someone would stir up old abandonment fears. Recognizing those connections gave me options. I could either react from the old wound or respond from the present moment.

There is also a spiritual element to this work. I believe we are not meant to live our entire lives imprisoned by past pain. Whatever name you use for the divine, whether you say God, the universe, or something else entirely, there is a higher calling toward peace. That peace is not passive. It requires courage. It requires self-examination. It requires humility.

Learning to forgive was part of my process. Forgiveness did not mean excusing what happened. It meant releasing the grip that those events had on my daily emotions. I had to forgive my mother for her addiction and her actions, even if I never fully understood them. I had to forgive my father for loving alcohol more than he loved showing up consistently. I had to forgive myself for the years I spent reacting from unresolved hurt.

When you forgive, you are not saying the pain was acceptable. You are saying that you refuse to let it dictate the rest of your life. That decision is powerful. It softens the internal landscape. It allows space for compassion, not only toward others, but toward yourself.

Anger often convinces you that you are strong because you are loud. True strength is quieter. It is the ability to sit with discomfort without exploding. It is the discipline to respond thoughtfully when everything inside you wants to lash out. It is the willingness to do internal work instead of blaming the entire world.

You do not have to live the rest of your life as an angry person. Your past may explain your reactions, but it does not excuse them indefinitely. There is help available. There are tools. There are practices that can calm your nervous system and reshape your patterns.

I am not sharing my story to shame anyone. I am sharing it because I lived it. I know what it feels like to see red. I know what it feels like to regret words spoken in heat. I also know what it feels like to experience the freedom that comes from finally understanding why you were so angry in the first place.

The anger beneath the anger deserves your attention. When you gently uncover it and tend to the wounds underneath, something shifts. The fire that once burned destructively begins to warm instead of scorch. Peace becomes possible, not because life stops challenging you, but because you have learned how to face those challenges without losing yourself.

8

Daily Practices That Calm the Fire

By the time I reached a place of awareness about my anger, I understood something very clearly. Insight alone is not enough. Knowing why you are angry does not automatically make you calm. Understanding your triggers does not prevent them from being activated. If change is going to last, it must be supported by daily practices that retrain your nervous system and reshape your habits. Awareness opens the door, but discipline walks you through it.

For me, that process began with something very simple. I learned how to slow down. That might sound obvious, but when you are used to reacting quickly, slowing down feels unnatural. My body was accustomed to tension. My thoughts were accustomed to speed. Pausing felt foreign. I started paying attention to my breathing. When I noticed my shoulders tightening or my jaw clenching, I would take a slow, intentional breath before responding. That single breath created space. It interrupted the automatic reaction that had ruled my life for years. In that pause, I regained authority over myself.

Reflection at the End of the Day

Another practice that transformed me was reflection at the end of the day. Instead of collapsing into bed and carrying unresolved emotions into the next morning, I began asking myself what had triggered me. I would sit quietly and replay moments that felt intense. I did not judge myself harshly. I simply observed. That observation helped me notice patterns. Certain tones, certain behaviors, certain words consistently activated me. Awareness gave me leverage.

During those evening reflections, I would ask deeper questions. What was I really feeling in that moment? Was it disrespect, or was it fear of being dismissed? Was it frustration, or was it a memory of feeling powerless? Taking the time to answer those questions prevented me from repeating the same emotional mistakes. It also helped me forgive myself for past reactions because I could see clearly where they came from.

Journaling as Emotional Release

Journaling became another safe outlet. Writing down what I felt prevented those emotions from exploding outward. There is something powerful about seeing your anger on paper. It makes it tangible. It removes it from your body and places it in front of you where you can evaluate it calmly. Many times, after writing everything out, I realized my reaction had been disproportionate to the situation.

I did not censor myself in those pages. I allowed myself to be honest, even when the thoughts were uncomfortable. Once they were written, I could examine them with compassion instead of shame. Over time, journaling became less about venting and more about growth. I began ending entries with a question: How could I have responded differently? That single question reshaped my behavior slowly and steadily.

Therapy and Professional Guidance

One of the most important decisions I ever made was to seek professional help. Enrolling in anger management was not easy for my ego. I was a business owner. I considered myself strong and capable. Sitting in a therapist's office and admitting I needed help required humility. It was one of the best investments I have ever made.

Therapy provided structure to my healing. It gave language to emotions I had never fully understood. It helped me identify triggers I would have overlooked on my own. Sometimes we need an outside perspective to reflect back what we cannot see clearly. There is no weakness in asking for help. There is strength in refusing to let pride keep you stuck.

Even now, I encourage anyone struggling with intense anger to consider professional guidance. Talking to a trained therapist can uncover layers that self reflection alone may not reach. Healing is not meant to be a solitary journey.

Meditation and Stillness

Meditation became a cornerstone of my emotional balance. Sitting quietly with my eyes closed was not something I grew up doing. At first, it felt awkward. My thoughts raced. My body wanted to move. Over time, I learned that meditation is not about stopping thoughts completely. It is about observing them without attaching to them.

Sometimes I would sit in my home in complete silence. Other times, I would sit on a park bench, just as I once heard Deepak Chopra describe, simply breathing and allowing the world to move around me. There is something grounding about sitting in public stillness. Watching people walk by, hearing distant traffic, feeling the air against your skin while remaining centered teaches your nervous system that you are safe.

Meditation taught me to separate myself from my thoughts. Instead of becoming every angry impulse that arose, I learned to watch it pass. That practice alone changed the intensity of my reactions more than I could have imagined.

Sound Healing and 432 Megahertz

Sound healing entered my life during a season when I was searching for deeper peace. I began listening to music tuned to 432 megahertz, which is often described as a frequency that promotes calm and harmony. Whether someone believes in the science behind it or simply experiences the effect, I can say personally that it soothes my nervous system.

There were nights when I would lie in bed with that frequency playing softly in the background. My breathing would slow. My thoughts would soften. The agitation that once felt constant would begin to dissolve. Sound has power. It influences mood, heartbeat, and emotional state. Incorporating calming frequencies into my routine became another gentle way to lower my baseline tension.

Gospel Music and Spiritual Uplift

Music has always spoken to my spirit. Gospel music, in particular, calms me in ways that are difficult to explain. When I play songs that remind me of God's presence and grace, something inside me settles. It shifts my focus from whatever frustration I am carrying to something greater than myself.

There have been moments when I felt anger rising, and instead of replaying the situation in my mind, I turned on a song that spoke to my faith. Singing along changes the atmosphere in the room and within my body. The lyrics remind me that I am not alone in my struggles and that peace is possible even in challenging moments.

Grounding and Putting My Feet in the Grass

One of the simplest practices that calms me is grounding. Taking off my shoes and placing my bare feet on the grass reconnects me to the earth in a very literal way. There is something profoundly stabilizing about feeling the ground beneath you. It reminds you that you are part of something larger.

When I feel overwhelmed, stepping outside and standing barefoot in the yard slows my thoughts. I focus on the sensation of the grass, the temperature of the air, the sound of birds or distant traffic. That sensory awareness pulls me out of my head and back into the present moment.

Sun Gazing and Light

Sunlight has always felt healing to me. I am careful and intentional, never staring directly at the sun during harsh daylight hours, but allowing myself to sit in early morning or late afternoon light has a calming effect. Closing my eyes and feeling the warmth on my face reminds me of life and renewal.

Light shifts mood. It reminds you that darkness is temporary. Incorporating sunlight into my daily rhythm has helped regulate not only my emotional state but also my overall well being.

Movement and Physical Release

Physical movement continues to play a role in my emotional health. Walking, stretching, or simply cleaning the house channels restless energy into something productive. Anger creates adrenaline. If that energy is not released, it lingers. Movement allows it to exit the body in a healthy way.

There have been times when a brisk walk prevented an argument. There have been mornings when stretching quietly reset my mood before the day began. Caring for the body is part of caring for the mind.

Compassionate Self Talk

I also had to change how I spoke to myself internally. My self talk used to be harsh. I would criticize myself for being triggered, which only added another layer of frustration. Over time, I learned to speak to myself with compassion. Instead of asking what was wrong with me, I began acknowledging that something old was being touched.

That gentle shift softened my reactions immediately. The more compassion I extended inward, the more patience I had outward.

Consistency Over Perfection

None of these practices eliminated anger completely. What they did was lower its intensity. They shortened the duration. They increased my ability to respond instead of react. Over time, the fire that once erupted uncontrollably became manageable.

The key is consistency. Doing these things once or twice will not transform you. Committing to them daily will. You are retraining patterns that may have been in place for decades. That requires patience and grace. Each calm response builds confidence. Each thoughtful pause strengthens your sense of control.

An angry world will not change overnight, but your internal world can. When you become someone who handles conflict with steadiness, people notice. Relationships shift. Communication improves. Your own body feels safer. Peace stops feeling like an abstract concept and becomes something you experience regularly.

Anger does not disappear by accident. It softens when you choose practices that calm your spirit and regulate your nervous system. Those practices are not dramatic. They are intentional. They are loving. They are consistent. Over time, they transform you from the inside out.

9

A Softer Strength

There was a time when I believed softness was weakness. I associated calmness with being overlooked. I thought that if I lowered my voice, people would not take me seriously. What I did not realize was that true strength is not loud. It is steady. It does not need to intimidate in order to be respected.

As I continued healing, I began noticing something surprising. When I responded calmly, people listened more carefully. When I spoke firmly without aggression, my words carried more weight. The same authority I once tried to enforce through fear began to emerge naturally through composure.

This transformation did not happen because life suddenly became easy. I still encountered difficult employees. I still faced challenging conversations. I still experienced moments that could have provoked anger. The difference was internal. I no longer needed to prove my power through volume or intensity. I had nothing to defend.

Learning this kind of strength requires humility. You have to admit that your previous approach was not serving you. You have to be willing to apologize when necessary. There were conversations I revisited with my children and former employees where I acknowledged that my reactions had been excessive. That honesty built bridges that anger had once burned.

Compassion also deepened. Once I understood the roots of my own anger, I began seeing others differently. The rude customer might be carrying unspoken pain. The disrespectful teenager might be navigating insecurities they cannot articulate. This does not excuse harmful behavior, but it helps you respond with clarity instead of retaliation.

The world feels harsh enough without us adding to it. Choosing a softer strength is not about becoming passive. It is about becoming intentional. It is about recognizing that your response shapes the environment around you. When you remain grounded in the face of tension, you change the energy of the room.

There is also something deeply healing about forgiving yourself. Many of us carry shame about past outbursts. We replay moments we wish we could redo. Growth does not require endless self punishment. It requires accountability followed by forward movement. The version of you who acted in anger was operating with limited tools. The version of you reading this now has more awareness.

Anger once defined me but no longer does. That shift did not erase my history. It transformed it into wisdom. My story now serves as a reminder that no one is stuck. No matter how explosive your past has been, you can become someone who leads with balance and clarity.

When someone closes this book, I want them to feel hope. I want them to know that anger is not a life sentence. I want them to understand that even if they were justified in their pain, they still have the power to choose peace. That peace begins inside and radiates outward.

A softer strength is available to you. It does not silence your voice. It refines it. It does not diminish your presence. It steadies it. It does not deny your pain. It honors it and moves beyond it.

An angry world needs individuals who have done their internal work. It needs people who have confronted their trauma and chosen healing. It needs men and women who understand that reacting impulsively is easy, but responding thoughtfully is powerful.

You can become one of those people. Not by pretending you were never angry, but by understanding why you were and choosing differently moving forward. That choice may not change the entire world overnight, but it will absolutely change yours.

10

I Declare War

In earlier chapters, I've shared openly about the years I lived with a very bad temper. I wasn't proud of it, but I also didn't fully understand it. I spent an enormous amount of energy fighting external battles. Arguments over differences of opinion felt like personal attacks. Disrespect, whether real or perceived, felt intolerable. When I felt offended, I believed it was my responsibility to correct the other person immediately, even if doing so meant raising my voice, slamming doors, or saying things that permanently damaged the relationship. I would mentally declare war on people, convincing myself that cutting them off was strength. I rehearsed imaginary confrontations in my mind, replaying what I should have said, escalating the argument long after it had ended, tightening my jaw and furrowing my brow until my own body carried the consequences of a fight that only existed in my head.

That kind of living is exhausting. It drains you physically

and emotionally. When anger becomes your primary defense, your world begins to feel like a battlefield. Everyone looks like a potential opponent. Every disagreement feels like a threat. Meanwhile, the real issue often goes untouched. The deeper wounds, the abandonment, the grief, the unresolved trauma, remain unaddressed while we focus all of our energy on external enemies.

At some point, I realized something that changed everything for me. The real war was never with other people. The real war was within.

The anger I projected outward was being fueled by an internal voice that I had never challenged. That voice whispered narratives about rejection, disrespect, and betrayal long before anyone else had done anything. It told me I was being attacked when sometimes I was simply being corrected. It convinced me that intensity was power and that domination was protection. That inner dialogue had been shaped by my past, by abandonment, by loss, by trauma I had not yet processed. Without realizing it, I had allowed that internal voice to control my reactions.

In this book, we are talking about root causes of anger. This is one of them. The mind creates stories, and when those stories go unchecked, they can ignite explosive reactions. Some people call that voice the ego. Some refer to it in spiritual terms. Others simply call it negative self-talk. The label is not important. What matters is recognizing that not every thought you think is true, and not every emotional surge deserves immediate expression.

When I finally understood that, I knew I needed to declare war, but not on my staff, not on my daughter, not on strangers, and not on the world. I needed to declare war on the unchecked internal narratives that were feeding my anger.

That declaration did not look dramatic. It looked intentional.

It meant catching the thought that said, "She's disrespecting you on purpose," and pausing long enough to ask whether that was actually true. It meant interrupting the belief that I had to win every disagreement to maintain authority. It meant confronting the deeper fear underneath the anger, the fear of being dismissed, abandoned, or made to feel small again.

The internal enemy thrives in silence and speed. When you never slow down long enough to examine your thinking, it continues to run your life. Many of us are unaware of how often we tell ourselves stories that inflame our emotions. A simple mistake by someone else becomes proof that no one respects you. A disagreement becomes confirmation that you are being attacked. A teenager's attitude becomes evidence that you are losing control. These interpretations may feel real, but they are filtered through old wounds.

Declaring war on that internal enemy means choosing awareness over impulse. It means understanding that anger often begins as a thought long before it becomes an outburst. If you can catch the thought, you can soften the reaction. If you can challenge the narrative, you can change the outcome.

Winning this war does not mean suppressing your emotions. It does not mean pretending you are never hurt or offended. It means refusing to let unexamined thoughts dictate destructive behavior. It means taking responsibility for your mental patterns instead of blaming everyone around you for how you feel.

There was a time when I believed my anger was caused entirely by other people's behavior. Now I understand that while people can trigger us, they do not control us. The trigger only works if something inside is already wounded. That realization was humbling. It forced me to stop pointing outward and start looking inward.

The true battle is in the mind. Mastering your reactions begins with mastering your thoughts. You cannot control every situation, but you can learn to control the meaning you assign to it. You can choose which thoughts to entertain and which to dismiss. You can decide whether a moment escalates or diffuses.

Persistent negative thinking patterns are far more damaging than most external conflicts. When you repeatedly tell yourself that you are disrespected, unloved, or threatened, your nervous system remains on high alert. Your body begins to live in fight mode. Over time, that constant state of internal warfare spills into your relationships, your health, and your peace of mind.

Declaring war in this context is not about aggression. It is about commitment. It is a decision that you will no longer allow unresolved pain to masquerade as justified rage. It is a promise that you will examine your triggers instead of defending them. It is the courage to say, "I will not let my past dictate my present reactions."

One of the first steps in this internal war is identification. What does your inner voice say when you are angry? Does it tell you that you are always being wronged? Does it exaggerate the offense? Does it replay old memories and blend them with the current situation? Has it convinced you that intensity equals strength?

Take a moment to reflect honestly. What has your internal dialogue been repeatedly telling you? What conclusions have you accepted without question? Which of those beliefs are rooted in past hurt rather than present reality?

You cannot dismantle what you refuse to see.

When you begin challenging that internal voice, something shifts. External enemies lose some of their power because you are no longer fueling the fire from within. Conflicts become conversations instead of battles. Disagreements stop feeling like threats to your identity. The world feels less hostile because your inner world is no longer at war.

In an angry world, it is easy to justify staying reactive. It can even feel empowering. But true strength is found in restraint, reflection, and self-mastery. The greatest victory you will ever achieve is not defeating someone else in an argument. It is gaining control over the impulses that once controlled you.

Declare war, yes, but declare it wisely. Declare it against the unchecked narratives that inflame your anger. Declare it against the wounds that have been running your reactions. Declare it against the belief that you are powerless over your own emotional responses.

When you win that internal battle, you do not just calm your temper. You reclaim your life.

11

When the World Feels Like It's Burning

There comes a point in your healing where your focus shifts from your personal anger to the anger you see everywhere around you. Once you begin calming the fire within yourself, you cannot help but notice how much of it is still raging in the world. Social media arguments that escalate into cruelty. Strangers fighting at concerts and sporting events. Road rage incidents that turn deadly. Families divided over politics, religion, or pride. It can feel overwhelming.

There was a time when I contributed to that energy without even realizing it. I added heat to conversations. I defended myself fiercely. I reacted quickly. Now, when I see public outrage, I recognize it differently. I see pain. I see unprocessed trauma. I see people who were never taught how to regulate their emotions. I see adults who were once wounded children.

An angry world is not created overnight. It is built slowly through generations of people who never addressed their own hurt. Trauma passes silently from parent to child, from household to household, until it becomes culture. When anger is normalized, it becomes contagious. One explosive response invites another. One insult invites retaliation. The cycle continues.

What I have come to understand is that collective healing begins with individual responsibility. We often look at the state of the world and feel powerless. We shake our heads at the violence. We criticize the chaos. We complain about the hostility. Rarely do we pause and ask ourselves what role we are playing in the emotional temperature of our communities.

If you want the world to be calmer, you must become calmer. If you want relationships to be healthier, you must model emotional health. If you want your children to regulate their emotions, they must see you regulating yours. Change is not theoretical. It is behavioral.

That realization gave me a new sense of purpose. My healing was no longer just about my peace. It became about what I contribute to every room I enter. When I walk into a space, I now ask myself whether I am bringing tension or stability. That awareness alone has transformed how I speak, how I listen, and how I respond.

Anger often feels justified in a world that is unfair. There are real injustices. There are real wounds. There are real betrayals. None of that disappears simply because you choose peace. What changes is your method. Instead of responding with destructive intensity, you respond with measured strength. Instead of escalating conflict, you seek resolution.

You may not be able to change global events. You can change your household. You can change your workplace. You can change your immediate circle. Those smaller shifts create ripples. Imagine if every individual committed to understanding the root of their anger instead of projecting it outward. The atmosphere of society would shift dramatically.

There is also something deeply freeing about refusing to participate in unnecessary outrage. Not every comment deserves a response. Not every disagreement requires a battle. Choosing not to engage in every provocation protects your energy and your mental health. It does not make you weak. It makes you wise.

When I think about the little girl I once was, the one who carried abandonment and grief silently, I realize she never wanted to grow into an angry adult. She wanted safety. She wanted love. She wanted stability. Beneath every angry person is someone who once wanted those same things.

Extending compassion to others does not mean allowing abuse. Boundaries are still necessary. Accountability still matters. What changes is the spirit in which you operate. You can enforce boundaries without cruelty. You can disagree without hatred. You can stand firm without exploding.

An angry world does not have to remain that way. The temperature lowers one person at a time. Every time you choose reflection over reaction, you contribute to a different atmosphere. Every time you apologize instead of justify, you model humility. Every time you breathe before responding, you interrupt a cycle that may have been running for generations.

The world may feel like it is burning at times. Your responsibility is not to add fuel. It is to become someone who carries water.

12

Peace Is a Decision

If there is one truth I want you to carry with you after reading this book, it is this: anger is not your identity. It may have been your habit. It may have been your shield. It may have felt like your personality for years. It is not who you are at your core.

You are not defined by the worst reaction you ever had. You are not permanently labeled by the seasons when you could not control your temper. You are a human being who has experienced pain, and pain can distort behavior. Once you understand that, the door to change opens wider than you may have ever believed possible.

Peace is not something that simply arrives one day as a gift. It is a decision you make repeatedly. It is a choice you reaffirm in moments of provocation. It is a commitment to growth even when your pride wants to defend old patterns. Choosing peace does not mean you will never feel angry again. It means you will handle that anger differently.

You have more control than you think. There was a time when I believed my reactions were automatic and unavoidable. I now know that there is always a split second between stimulus and response. In that space lives your power. In that space lives your future. One choice in that moment can change the trajectory of a relationship, a career, or a life.

There are people whose lives shifted permanently because they reacted impulsively in a heated second. There are others whose lives improved dramatically because they paused, breathed, and chose restraint. That difference is not about luck. It is about awareness and discipline.

You may have experienced trauma that would make anyone angry. You may have endured betrayal, abandonment, injustice, or neglect. None of that disqualifies you from healing. None of that condemns you to remain reactive. Your past explains your patterns, but it does not control your destiny.

When I look back at the woman I used to be, I feel compassion rather than shame. She was doing the best she could with the tools she had. The version of me now has more tools. I have therapy. I have meditation. I have grounding practices. I have faith. I have self awareness. Most importantly, I have the humility to admit when I am wrong and the strength to correct it.

You can build those tools too. You can slow down. You can breathe. You can journal. You can seek help. You can pray. You can sit in stillness. You can walk barefoot in the grass and remember that you are part of something larger than your current frustration. You can choose to break generational cycles of explosive behavior.

Peace does not require perfection. It requires intention. There will be moments when you stumble. There will be days when old triggers resurface. That does not mean you have failed. It means you are human. The difference now is that you know what to do. You know how to return to center.

Imagine what your life could look like if anger no longer dictated your reactions. Imagine conversations that end in understanding instead of silence. Imagine your children observing your calm strength. Imagine your body no longer bracing for conflict at every turn. That life is possible.

An angry world needs healed individuals. It needs men and women who have confronted their wounds and decided not to pass them forward. It needs leaders who speak firmly without cruelty. It needs parents who model regulation instead of rage. It needs business owners who lead with steadiness instead of fear.

You have the power to become that person. Not by denying your history, but by transforming it into wisdom. Not by pretending you were never angry, but by understanding why you were and choosing differently now.

The final decision rests with you. You can continue reacting the way you always have, or you can pause and take responsibility for the next moment. That next moment matters. It may feel small, but it is the seed of your future.

I once lived as an angry woman who did not understand the roots of her fire. Today, I live as someone who has learned to sit with discomfort, breathe through triggers, and respond with clarity. If I can make that shift after everything I have experienced, so can you.

Peace is not passive. It is powerful and intentional. It is available to you right now.

Choose it.

13

Conclusion

If you have made it to the end of this book, I want you to pause for a moment and acknowledge something important. You are here because some part of you is ready. Ready to stop living on edge. Ready to stop explaining away your reactions. Ready to stop carrying anger like armor. That readiness alone tells me you are stronger than you think.

Anger may have protected you once. It may have helped you survive environments that were chaotic, unsafe, or un-predictable. It may have given you a sense of control when everything else felt out of control. I understand that deeply. I lived that way for years. But what once protected you can eventually imprison you. What once kept people from hurting you can slowly push away the very love and stability you deserve.

There is something incredibly powerful about realizing that you are not doomed to repeat the same emotional patterns forever. You are not required to stay the person you had to become in order to survive your childhood. You are not obligated to continue reacting from wounds that were never your fault. The past may explain your anger, but it does not own your future.

You have more authority over your life than you have been led to believe. In every heated moment, there is a choice. In every trigger, there is a split second where you can decide whether to escalate or to breathe. That second may feel small, but it carries enormous weight. Entire relationships can shift because of how you handle one intense exchange. Entire legacies can change because you chose peace instead of pride.

This world does not need more rage. It does not need more people proving points at the expense of connection. It does not need more explosions that leave everyone wounded. What it needs are individuals courageous enough to confront their own pain and transform it into wisdom. What it needs are parents who decide the cycle stops with them. What it needs are leaders who understand that strength and calm are not opposites.

Healing your anger does not mean you will never feel upset again. It means you will no longer be ruled by it. It means your emotions will inform you instead of control you. It means you will respond from clarity instead of chaos. That shift changes everything.

I want you to envision a version of yourself who is steady under pressure. A version of you who can handle disrespect without losing dignity. A version of you who addresses conflict without becoming destructive. That version is not imaginary. That version is possible. That version is already forming the moment you decide that anger will no longer define you.

You have survived enough. You have carried enough. You have reacted enough. Now it is time to live differently. Now it is time to experience what it feels like to walk into a room without tension in your chest. Now it is time to build relationships rooted in respect rather than fear. Now it is time to feel proud of how you handle yourself.

The world may still be loud. People may still provoke. Situations may still test you. None of that changes the fact that you can choose your response. That choice is your power. That power is your freedom.

From fire to freedom is not just a phrase. It is a journey. It is the journey from reacting to responding, from exploding to reflecting, from wounding to healing. It is the journey I have walked, and it is one you can walk too.

You are not an angry person. You are a person who has felt pain, and pain, when understood, can become purpose. Pain, when processed, can become compassion and love. Pain, when healed, can become strength.

Choose peace and growth. Choose to be the one who breaks the cycle. The world will feel different when you do.

Also by Bri Reece

SaBrina Fisher Reece understands what it means to keep going without applause.

For more than twenty six years, she built one of the most influential braiding salons and schools in Los Angeles, Braids By SaBrina, earning recognition throughout California as The Braid Queen. Her name was on the door, her reputation was on the line, and her success was self built. Behind the achievements, however, was a quieter truth. Much of her journey was navigated without consistent support, validation, or encouragement from others.

SaBrina's life has been shaped by early abandonment, profound loss, and the slow, intentional development of self trust. Those experiences taught her that confidence on the outside does not always mean peace on the inside, and that real strength is often learned when you are forced to become your own support system.

Today, SaBrina is an author, speaker, and guide devoted to emotional growth, self mastery, and inner alignment. She is the author of multiple transformational works, including *My Spiritual Smile: Tools for Mental and Emotional Transformation, Your Mind Is Magic, Perfectly Positive: How to Stay Positive When Life Is Not Perfect, Spiritual Balance: Aligning Mind, Body, and Energy in Everyday Life, Living Life on a Higher Frequency, How to Get Exactly What You Want From God, Kicking Depression in the Butt, Self Sabotage, Become Your Own Cheerleader, Family Fun Night Cookbook, When I Say I Am, How to Make More Money in 2026,* and *Over Fifty and Still Fine, Looking to Date Again.* Each book reflects a chapter of her own evolution and healing.

Now residing in New Mexico, SaBrina continues her work through writing, sound healing practices, and helping others bring their literary dreams to life through In59Seconds Publishing Co. She consistently reminds readers that there is no single path to peace, only the courage to walk your own.

Her message is simple and unwavering.

Sometimes the most important applause you will ever receive is the one you give yourself.

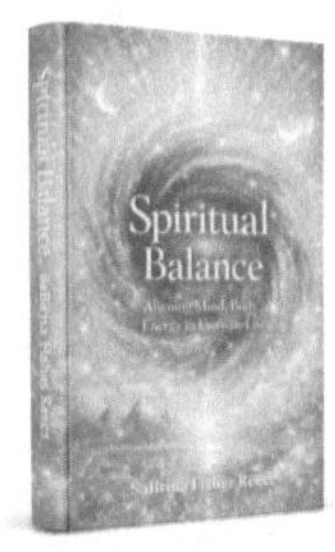

Spiritual Balance

Aligning Mind, Body, and Energy in Everyday Life is a grounded, insightful guide for anyone seeking clarity, emotional stability, and deeper alignment in a fast-moving world.

In this book, SaBrina Fisher Reece explores the truth that many people sense but struggle to articulate: life becomes chaotic when our inner energies are out of balance. Drawing from spiritual principles, lived experience, and practical awareness, *Spiritual Balance* breaks down how the mind, body, and energetic self are deeply interconnected—and how neglecting one inevitably affects the others.

This book reframes common spiritual concepts in a way that is accessible, realistic, and applicable to everyday life. Readers will learn that masculine and feminine energies are not tied to gender, but are universal forces present within every person. When these energies are balanced, we experience greater peace, confidence, emotional regulation, and healthier relationships. When they are not, stress, confusion, and emotional exhaustion take over.

Rather than offering abstract philosophy, *Spiritual Balance* provides readers with a new way of understanding themselves. It encourages self-awareness, intentional living, and emotional responsibility without shame or perfectionism. Topics include emotional balance, energetic boundaries, spiritual awareness, self-worth, and the role of unseen forces in shaping our daily experiences.

This book is for readers who know there is more to life than what can be seen, measured, or explained logically—

but who also want something practical, grounded, and honest. *Spiritual Balance* meets spirituality where real life happens: in relationships, work, healing, growth, and everyday decisions.

By aligning mind, body, and energy, readers are guided toward a more peaceful, empowered, and intentional way of living— one that honors both the human experience and the spiritual truth beneath it.

Is This Why They Burned The Books? (EBOOK)

Buried Wisdom from the Past

What if the most powerful knowledge was never destroyed... only buried?

Across history, libraries have burned, philosophers have been silenced, and ancient civilizations have disappeared. Yet fragments of their wisdom continue to surface in unexpected places. In sacred geometry carved into stone. In healing traditions rooted in the earth. In philosophies that challenge us to master the mind. In spiritual teachings that insist the kingdom is within.

In *Is This Why They Burned the Books?*, Bri Reece takes readers on a deeply personal and thought provoking journey through ancient Egypt, Peru, and Greece, exploring the possibility that humanity once understood more about consciousness, energy, and inner power than we acknowledge today.

Drawing from travel experiences inside the Great Pyramid of Giza, meditation above Machu Picchu, and reflections in Delphi and Meteora, this book bridges ancient civilizations with modern self awareness. It asks bold but balanced questions:

What did our ancestors know about the mind? Why do certain ideas about human potential keep resurfacing across centuries? Are we operating at only a fraction of our true capacity? What does evolving to a higher self actually look like?

This is not a conspiracy book. It is a curiosity book. It does not attack religion. It expands perspective. It does not claim certainty. It invites exploration.

Through thoughtful reflection on ancient wisdom, energy, grounding, inner discipline, and the vastness of the universe, Bri

Reece offers readers something far more valuable than answers. She offers responsibility. The responsibility to think deeply, to seek humbly, and to remember that human potential is far from exhausted.

If you have ever felt that there is more to this life than routine and repetition... If you are a seeker who questions without arrogance...

If you sense that buried wisdom is waiting to be rediscovered...

This book is for you. The fire may have burned the pages.

But the wisdom remains.

Living Life on a Higher Frequency Daily Steps to Raising Your Personal Vibration: is an invitation to remember who you truly are at your core: energy in motion.

Everything in life carries a frequency, including your thoughts, emotions, words, and choices. When you feel joy, gratitude, and peace, your energy expands and rises. When you feel anger, fear, resentment, or despair, your vibration lowers and contracts. This book teaches you how to recognize those shifts and consciously choose alignment instead of reaction.

Through spiritual insight, personal experience, and practical reflection, SaBrina Fisher Reece shows how emotional awareness is not just self improvement, it is energetic mastery. You will learn how to identify low frequency states before they take control, how to shift your internal energy without denying your humanity, and how to return to peace even when life feels chaotic.

This is not about pretending everything is perfect or bypassing pain. It is about understanding that emotions are signals, not destinations. You may not always control what happens to you, but you can control how long you remain in anger, sadness, or fear. That choice determines the quality of your life.

Inside these pages, you will explore how love, gratitude, forgiveness, stillness, and intention naturally elevate your vibration, while resentment, ego, and emotional reactivity quietly drain it. You will also discover how energy influences your relationships, your finances, your health, and your sense of purpose.

Living at a higher frequency is not mystical or unreachable.

It is a daily practice of awareness, alignment, and self respect. When you shift your energy, your perspective changes. When your perspective changes, your life begins to follow.

This book is for anyone ready to stop being controlled by their emotions and start living from a place of peace, clarity, and conscious choice.

Because when you raise your vibration, you do not just change how you feel.

You change how you experience life.

How to Make More and Work Less
A Guide to Increasing Your Income Quickly
is not another hustle book filled with recycled advice or unrealistic promises. It is a grounded, compassionate guide for people who have worked hard, played by the rules, and still found themselves facing financial uncertainty in a changing economy.

Written from lived experience, this book speaks directly to adults who are tired of surviving and ready to build a life that includes peace, stability, and abundance. With honesty and warmth, Bri Reece shows readers how to stop trading endless hours for diminishing returns and start creating income through their existing skills, knowledge, and life experience.

Blending practical insight with heartfelt encouragement, this book explores how to turn what you already know into income, how old school marketing still works in a digital world, and how teaching, writing, and speaking can create leverage without burnout. Most importantly, it addresses the mindset shift required to move from constant stress to sustainable freedom, reminding readers that struggle may have been part of their journey, but it was never meant to be their forever.

This book is for anyone who has worried quietly about bills, felt overlooked by a changing economy, or wondered if it was too late to start again. It offers clarity, hope, and real options for making more money while reclaiming time, dignity, and joy.

If you are ready to believe in possibility again and build a life that supports you instead of drains you, this book meets you exactly where you are and gently shows you what is still possible.

Over 50 and Still Fine - Looking to Date Again

Dating after 50 is not for the faint of heart, but it *can* be healing, hilarious, and empowering.

Over 50 and Still Fine is an honest, relatable, and uplifting guide for anyone stepping back into the dating world after heartbreak, divorce, long-term relationships, or years of choosing themselves first. With humor and raw transparency, SaBrina Fisher Reece shares real stories, lessons learned, and the emotional growth that comes with midlife dating.

This book is not about pretending dating is easy, it's about navigating the awkward moments, the red flags, the hope, the disappointment, and the unexpected joy with wisdom and self-respect. SaBrina reminds readers that healing doesn't mean shutting down, and confidence doesn't come from being chosen, it comes from knowing your worth.

Inside, you'll laugh, reflect, and recognize yourself as you explore:

Dating with boundaries instead of desperation

Healing old wounds while opening your heart again

Recognizing patterns and avoiding emotional burnout

Choosing peace, clarity, and self-love at every stage

If you're over 50, still fine, and considering love again, this book is your reminder that your story isn't over, your heart isn't broken beyond repair, and it's never too late to date with intention, humor, and confidence.

Kicking Depression in the Butt

Kicking Depression in the Butt: How to Battle The Internal Enemy and Win is a raw, faith-infused, and deeply practical guide for anyone who is tired of surviving in silence and ready to reclaim their life.

Drawing from her own lived experiences with trauma, abandonment, loss, and depression, SaBrina Fisher Reece invites readers into an honest conversation about what depression really feels like,and how to fight back. This book does not minimize pain or offer shallow positivity. Instead, it helps readers recognize depression as an internal enemy, interrupt destructive thought cycles, and rebuild their inner world with intention, truth, and daily tools that actually work.

Through personal storytelling, spiritual insight, and mindset-shifting strategies, SaBrina shows readers how to stop identifying with their darkest thoughts and begin designing a life that protects their peace. She addresses the realities of trauma, triggers, boundaries, faith, therapy, medication, and personal responsibility, offering a balanced approach that honors both professional support and inner work.

Kicking Depression in the Butt is for the person who keeps showing up while quietly falling apart. It is for those who smile while suffering, who feel strong on the outside but exhausted on the inside. Most of all, it is a reminder that depression may visit, but it does not get to stay, and it does not get to become your identity.

This book is not about perfection. It's about progress. It's about learning how to fight for your mind, your peace, and your future, one thought, one choice, and one day at a time.

Because as long as you have breath in your body, your story is not over, and you still have the power to kick depression in the butt.

Second By Second
Daily Tools to Co-Create a Great Life:

Second by Second: Daily Tools to Co-Create a Great Life explores the concept that human beings actively shape their reality through thought, emotion, and intentional focus.

Drawing from spiritual principles, practical psychology, and personal experience, Bri Reece presents a structured approach to conscious co-creation. The book emphasizes the power of visualization, emotional alignment, and disciplined thought management as daily tools for personal transformation.

Through relatable stories and accessible instruction, readers learn how to:

Recognize and redirect limiting thought patterns

Use imagination as a creative instrument

Align emotion with desired outcomes

Integrate spiritual belief with personal responsibility

Bri Reece presents co-creation as a partnership between the individual and the divine, offering readers a framework for intentional living grounded in faith, awareness, and consistent practice.

This book is designed for readers interested in personal development, spirituality, mindset mastery, and practical tools for self-directed growth.

When I Say " I AM"

What you say after "I Am" has the power to shape your entire life.

In *When I Say "I Am"*, SaBrina Fisher Reece reveals the sacred and scientific power of spoken identity. Blending spiritual truth, biblical wisdom, and universal law, this transformational book teaches readers how their words are not just communication—but creation. Every "I Am" statement becomes a command to the subconscious, a signal to the universe, and a declaration to the spiritual realm.

Drawing from scripture, including God's revelation of "I AM" as the eternal source of being, SaBrina shows how the same creative force lives within each of us. Through emotionally moving insight, practical affirmations, and deep spiritual awareness, readers learn how to shift from fear-based language to faith-based declarations that activate healing, confidence, abundance, and purpose.

This book will help you: Break negative identity patterns Reprogram limiting beliefs Speak life instead of fear. Align your words with divine promise

Use "I Am" as a daily tool for transformation More than motivation, *When I Say "I Am"* is a blueprint for conscious creation. It reminds you that your voice is powerful, your identity is sacred, and your words are always working-either for you or against you.

If you are ready to stop speaking survival and start speaking destiny, this book will show you how to command your life with intention, faith, and divine authority-one "I Am" at a time.

Self-Sabotage

Learning Not to Be Your Own Worst Enemy is a powerful exploration of the quiet ways we work against ourselves without even realizing it. This book is not about blame or shame. It is about awareness, compassion, and the courage to interrupt patterns that were formed in survival but no longer serve who you are becoming.

Many of us carry invisible wounds from trauma, abandonment, loss, or repeated disappointment. Over time, those wounds shape our thoughts, reactions, and choices. We second-guess ourselves. We push away love. We stay stuck in cycles we say we want to escape. We call it fear, timing, or bad luck, but often it is something deeper. It is self-sabotage rooted in pain that was never given space to heal.

Through reflection, emotional insight, and spiritual grounding, SaBrina Fisher Reece invites readers to look inward with honesty instead of judgment. She explores how self-sabotage shows up in relationships, self-worth, decision-making, and personal growth, not as a character flaw, but as a learned response to past hurt. With clarity and compassion, this book helps readers understand why they do what they do, and more importantly, how to choose differently.

This is a book for anyone who has felt stuck in their own patterns, exhausted by repeating the same lessons, or frustrated by knowing what they want but feeling unable to reach it. It is for those who are ready to stop fighting themselves and start working with their mind, emotions, and energy instead of against them.

Self-Sabotage does not promise quick fixes or surface-level

motivation. It offers something far more meaningful. Awareness that leads to freedom. Understanding that leads to choice. And self-love that is rooted in truth, not perfection.

If you are ready to stop being your own worst enemy and begin becoming your strongest ally, this book will meet you exactly where you are.

The World Is Ready

A Gentle Awakening to Sound, Energy, and the Spiritual Self is a compassionate invitation for those who sense there is more to life than what they were taught to see, yet still wish to honor their faith, their upbringing, and their reverence for God.

Written for readers raised within structured religious traditions, this book offers a safe and respectful bridge into spiritual practices that support balance, healing, and inner awareness. It reassures the reader that exploring sound healing, breathwork, meditation, grounding, and energy awareness is not a betrayal of faith, but a natural expansion of it.

Through deeply personal experiences, including recovery from major surgery supported by sound, private sound healing sessions, and sacred encounters in spiritual sites across the world, the author gently illustrates how ancient practices and modern understanding meet. From binaural beats and tuning forks to healing crystals, chakras, breath as life force, and the quiet power of the mind, each chapter unfolds with warmth, clarity, and emotional honesty.

This book does not preach, persuade, or pressure. Instead, it speaks softly to the soul, honoring curiosity while dissolving fear. It recognizes that spirituality does not belong to one religion, culture, or language, but lives within the shared human experience of seeking peace, connection, and meaning.

The World Is Ready is for anyone who has ever felt drawn to spiritual exploration but hesitated out of loyalty, doubt, or uncertainty. It affirms that spiritual practices are not witchcraft or rebellion, but tools of awareness that help us return to balance, regulate the nervous system, and remember our true nature.

This is not a call to abandon belief. It is an invitation to remember who you are. The world is ready.